SAMMIE'S TAIL
My Story Of Rescue

By Stasie Fishman

Sammie's Tail® is a story about a special needs cat and how she found her furrrever home.

Sammie's

T OLERANCE FOR

A NIMALS

I NSPIRES

L OVE

I don't remember much about what happened to me, so I can only start here.

I'm a unique breed of cat called Bombay, and I have special needs. I don't see well out of my left eye. It looks like I see through a gray cloud. It's tough for me to be all alone outside.

I'm also a black cat, and sometimes black cats aren't understood. Black cats are loving and playful. We're very close to our families and thankful for the love we receive.

I'm very small compared to other cats, and a couple of years ago, I felt lonely, cold, and scared. One particularly cold winter, I started hanging around a certain house.

I found a piece of pizza in some spilled garbage and carried it around with me outside the house. There were no dogs, and it was a quiet house, so I often huddled under the car to stay warm.

Then, one day, all of a sudden, there was a bowl of food and water. Wow! I was so happy!

I was *so* hungry I didn't even mind a person watching me eat. My dish kept moving each day until it ended up in the backyard. I felt safer there.

Soon, I started to eat in the backyard every day, twice a day. There was a house for me to go to if it rained.

I preferred to hang under the tree in a corner by the fence and get a bit wet. From this spot, they could see me from their window and then come out to bring food. The lady sat there on the back steps while I ate, and she tossed me some treats. Yum! I was excited!

The winter was over, and it was almost summer. I liked the person, the lady. There was a man, too. I eventually learned to trust them both and let them pet me. I had some memories of being petted before, but that was all I could recall. Their gentleness reminded me that people could be kind. In fact, I loved the warmth of their hands, especially under my chin and on my back.

I loved, loved, loved it! Purrrrrfect!

The weather was beginning to get colder, and one night, they invited me inside their house to eat. Wow! I felt nervous and called that place the "food room." I kept looking behind me to check that the door would stay open so I could leave if I wanted to.

But I kept coming back because the food was tasty and life was *so* good!

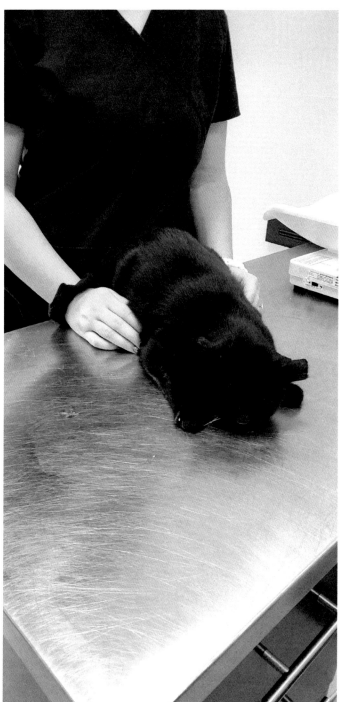

I enjoyed my visits for a while. Then, one day in October, I entered the food room, and the door closed behind me. They put me into a nice, cozy, safe little crate to sleep. Before I knew it, I was at a place with other animals and a doctor. I felt they were nice people who were giving me a check-up to make sure I was okay.

Before I knew it, I was back in the food room, eating the food I loved so much. Yummy!

The nice lady and man moved me into a small room, and I saw an open window with a screen. I wasn't sure if I should stay there. So, I climbed up and chewed a hole in the window screen, squeezed myself through the hole, and jumped down. I was back in the yard. I became hungry and started to miss the people. I sat in my favorite spot under the tree, looked up at the window, and waited for them.

The lady opened the door and called to me. I went up the steps and walked into the food room. Then, she closed the door behind me.

After a few months, I knew that was my home. I had yummy food, gentle people, and plenty of safe places to sleep. I was safe and happy—*so* happy! I walked around with my tail high in the shape of a question mark—a clear sign I was the happiest I could remember.

I learned my name was Sammie, and whenever they called, I came to them, as it was always good and happy.

It took a while to get used to my new life. I was still scared of some things that reminded me of my old life.

Now, I still don't like toys with long sticks, but I love to play with toy mice when they are left on the floor. I also like to sing to my dolly they gave me.

I have toys and different beds to sleep in. I love my life!

The lady and man are my new Mommy and Daddy. We are a happy family.

One day, I woke up and saw a black and white cat in my home…

My little family seemed to be growing! Wow!

The End.

Or, was it another new beginning?

Watch for Sammie's sister Bettinna

and her rescue story…

Bettinna, the Tablet Queen!

Bettinna	Freddie	Lucy
Ricky	Sylvia	Grayson

Meet Sammie's Family!

Look for their stories on

SammiesTail.com

Resources / How you can help

Contact your local shelters or cat rescue organizations in your area to donate whatever they need. Donate your time, find a local TNR, volunteer to help.

Donate! Adopt! Volunteer!

Thank you…

- To all the great people who help reduce the homeless cat population.

- To all who volunteer their time to help animals in shelters.

- To all who do TNR (Trap, Neuter & Release) to prevent more cats from being homeless and alone outside.

- To all who feed outside cats responsibly while making sure no more homeless kitties are alone.

- To all who reduce the number of cats euthanized.

- A special thank you to my friend Margaret, who fed cats outside and inspired me to do the same. If it weren't for her, I would not have my life enriched by my cat family: Sammie, Bettinna, Freddie, Lucy, Ricky, Sylvia, and Grayson.

- To Debbie De Louise—author and librarian—for her inspiration and guidance with her mystery cat storybooks. *DebbieDelouise.com*

- To Deborah Sevilla at Dream Believe Publish for helping me with formatting and bringing my dream to reality. *DreamBelievePublish.com*

- To Susan Healy—librarian and friend—for all her support and encouragement.

- To my cat family for their inspiration and bringing joy to my life.

Meet the Author

Stasie is a Long Island, New York author with a passion for animal and human rights who desires to create awareness of the homeless cat situation as well as tolerance for all animals and humans.

Since Stasie adopted Sammie seven years ago, her life has been enriched.

Stasie Fishman grew up without pets due to allergies in her family. She loved animals and adopted her neighbor's pets, especially a mutt dog named Simon, who was her "Lassie." Sammie, her sister Bettinna, and her outside siblings, Freddie, Lucy, Ricky, Sylvia, and Grayson, bring unconditional love and joy to Stasie's life.

Visit Stasie and her cat family at SammiesTail.com and follow them on Twitter, Facebook, and Instagram.

Spreading Love, Kindness, and Tolerance for all animals.

Sammie's T.A.I.L. = Tolerance for Animals Inspires Love

Shop for merchandise featuring your favorite cat at SammiesTail.com and take a souvenir home.

Sammies Tail

Sammie's Tail is a proud
promoter of animal rescue.

Manufactured by Amazon.ca
Bolton, ON

14742300R00024